T0353917

HOW CAN I HELP?

Roxy
the
butterfly

Frances Rodgers and **Ben Grisdale**

Written and illustrated by
Frances Rodgers and Ben Grisdale

Editor Abi Luscombe
Project Art Editor Charlotte Bull
Managing Editor Laura Gilbert
Publishing Manager Francesca Young
Publishing Coordinator Issy Walsh
Production Editor Abi Maxwell
Production Controller John Casey
Deputy Art Director Mabel Chan
Publishing Director Sarah Larter

First published in Great Britain in 2022
by Dorling Kindersley Limited
DK, One Embassy Gardens,
8 Viaduct Gardens, London, SW11 7BW

The authorised representative in the EEA is
Dorling Kindersley Verlag GmbH. Arnulfstr.
124, 80636 Munich, Germany

Copyright © 2022 Dorling Kindersley Limited
A Penguin Random House Company
10 9 8 7 6 5 4 3 2 1
001–326596–Apr/2022
All rights reserved.

A CIP catalogue record for this book
is available from the British Library.
ISBN: 978-0-2415-3450-2

Printed and bound in China

For the curious
www.dk.com

This book was made with Forest Stewardship
Council™ certified paper – one small step in
DK's commitment to a sustainable future.

For more information go to
www.dk.com/our-green-pledge

Hello, my name is Roxy.
I am a butterfly and
I need your help.

I start my life as a caterpillar.

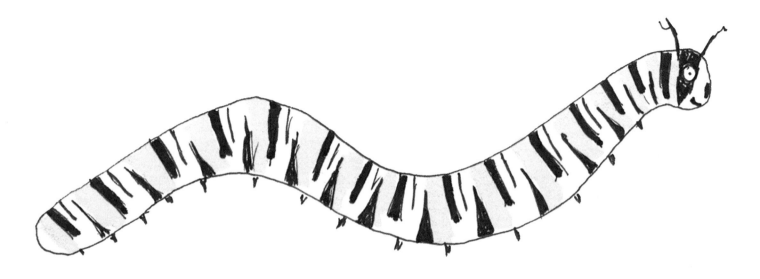

I go to sleep in my
chrysalis in a safe place.

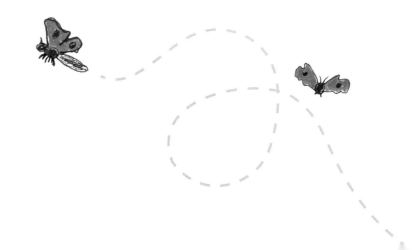

Then I begin to change.

ABRACADABRA

YAWN!

STRETCH!

When I wake up, I have
turned into a butterfly.

I like to feed on nectar found on the flowers in your garden.

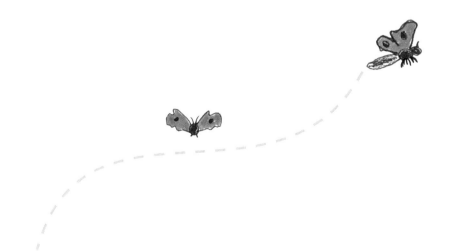

Nectar

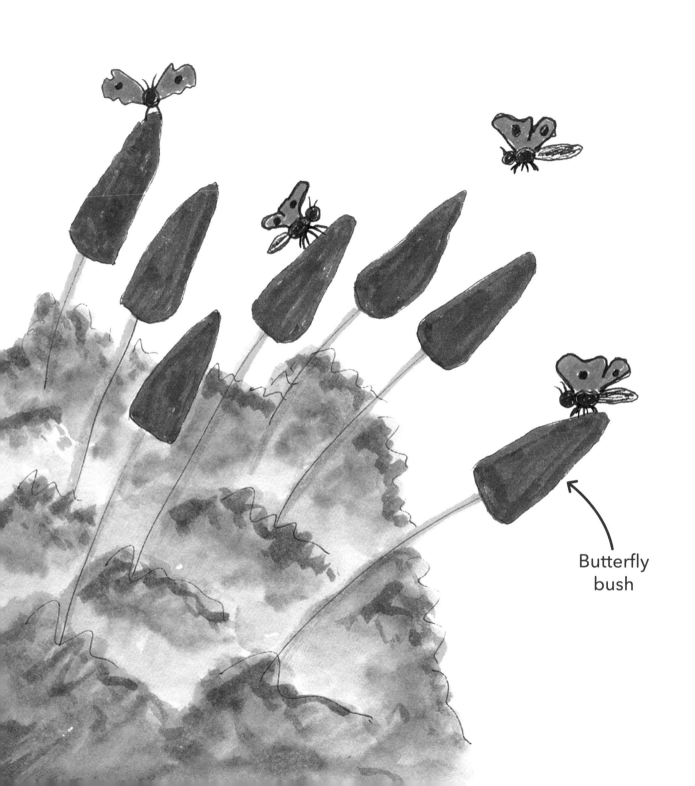

Butterfly
bush

Please plant lots of flowers
for me. My favourite plant
is called Butterfly bush.

I can taste through my feet.

When I get thirsty, I like
to drink juice from fruit.

Please put some old fruit out for me in your garden. I like apples, oranges, and bananas.

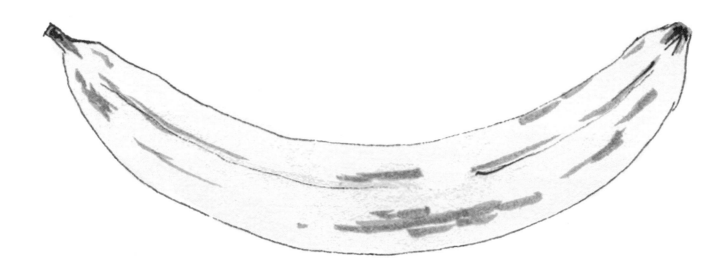

My tongue is a bit like a straw.

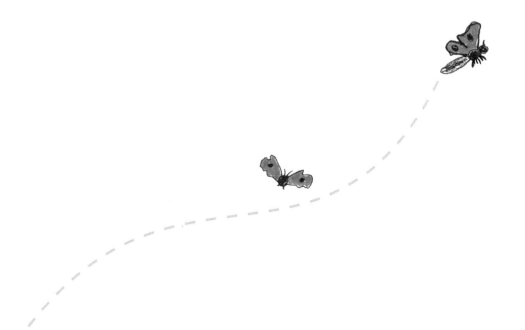

I get tired and need
somewhere to rest.

**Please build me a bug hotel
out of logs and wood.**

Thank you for all your help.

Why do we need to protect butterflies?

Butterflies, like Roxy, need to be protected. They can be found all around the world. Some types of butterflies have been around for a long time – at least 50 million years! However, many butterflies are endangered.

Scientists are worried because some of these wonderful, winged creatures appear to be dying out. That is why we need to do our bit to help them before it is too late!

Pollination

Some of the plants in your garden produce nectar which is a sweet, sugary liquid that many insects, including Roxy, like to eat. When butterflies land on flowers in your garden, they use their long, straw-like tongues (proboscises) to suck up the nectar. They also get pollen, an orange powder, stuck to their legs and body.

Phlox

This pollen is then carried to other flowers, which causes new seeds or fruit to grow. This process is called pollination. Butterflies, like Roxy, are important pollinators. Can you spot any in your garden?

Butterfly bush

Aster

Marigold

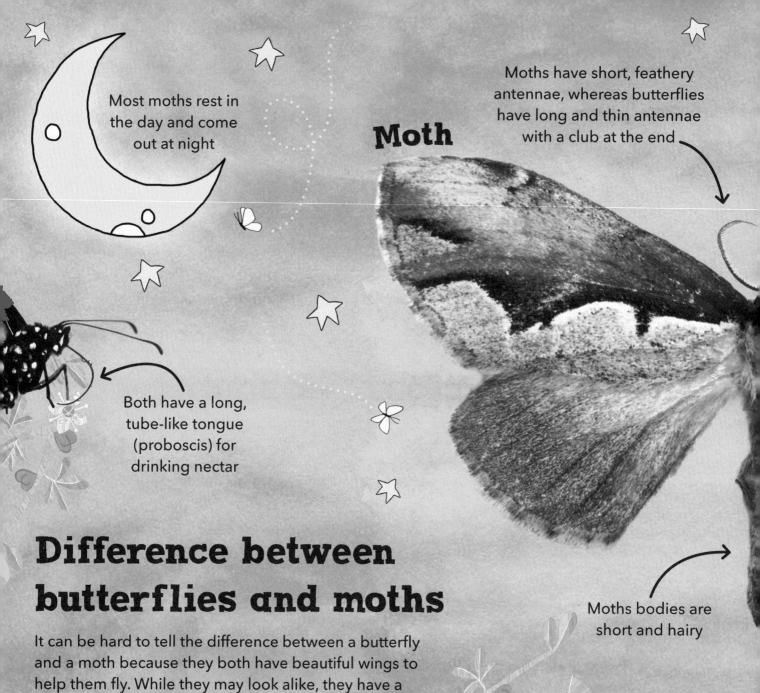

Most moths rest in the day and come out at night

Moths have short, feathery antennae, whereas butterflies have long and thin antennae with a club at the end

Moth

Both have a long, tube-like tongue (proboscis) for drinking nectar

Moths bodies are short and hairy

Difference between butterflies and moths

It can be hard to tell the difference between a butterfly and a moth because they both have beautiful wings to help them fly. While they may look alike, they have a few differences. Here are some things to look out for when searching for butterflies in your garden...

Butterflies tend to be more colourful than moths

Butterfly

Most butterflies rest at night and come out during the day

Both have wings that are covered in tiny scales. Moths wings are usually shorter while butterflies have larger wings

Butterflies rest with their wings closed and upright, whereas moths rest with their wings open and flat

Butterflies around the world

There are more than 250,000 species of spectacular butterflies and moths around the world. Which ones have you seen?

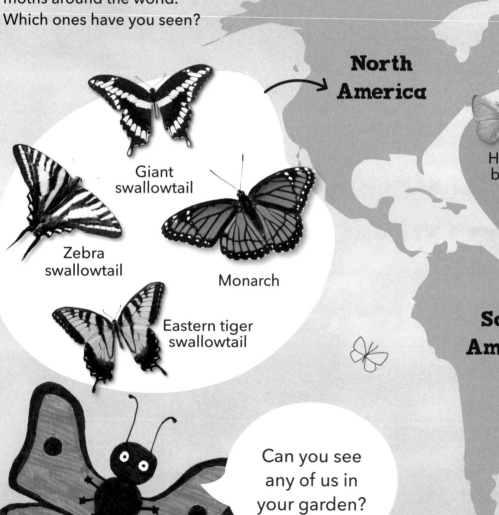

Giant swallowtail

Zebra swallowtail

Monarch

Eastern tiger swallowtail

Can you see any of us in your garden?

North America

South America

UK

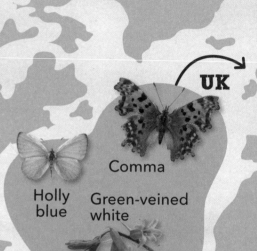

Comma

Holly blue

Green-veined white

Grecian shoemaker

Morpho helena

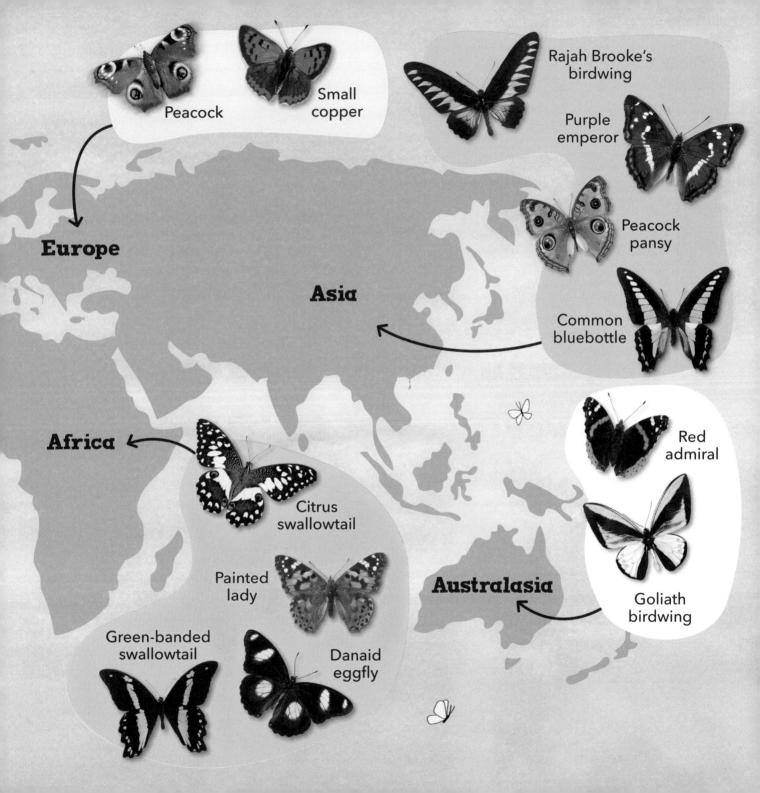

Peacock

Small copper

Europe

Rajah Brooke's birdwing

Purple emperor

Peacock pansy

Common bluebottle

Asia

Africa

Citrus swallowtail

Painted lady

Green-banded swallowtail

Danaid eggfly

Australasia

Red admiral

Goliath birdwing